Sam Sivell currently lives in Cambridgeshire with her husband and two children but is originally from Romford, Essex. She enjoys walking in the countryside and although she works full-time, she loves being at home with her family. Writing poetry has been a passion throughout her life which has helped her deal with some life-changing situations.

To all those people whose smile is purely a mask. One day you will walk with a spring in your step and feel at peace with yourself.

Sam Sivell

THE DARK CLOUD THAT OUTSHINES MY SUN

AUSTIN MACAULEY PUBLISHERS™

LONDON • CAMBRIDGE • NEW YORK • SHARJAH

A CIP catalogue record for this title is available from the British Library.

ISBN 9781528999953 (Paperback)
ISBN 9781528999960 (ePub e-book)

www.austinmacauley.com

First Published (2021)
Austin Macauley Publishers Ltd
25 Canada Square
Canary Wharf
London
E14 5LQ

To my family, for listening to many a late-night call, endless tears; thank you for being there when I needed you.

To my children, for keeping me sane, and for giving me a reason to get up and face each day without even knowing it.

To Alex, for showing me I am worthy and Angie, for putting up with me in the office over the years.

I love you all.

Contents

Preface

I have suffered with depression throughout various chapters of my life, normally a reaction to an event that has occurred. It has resulted in my days feeling dark but sometimes just a feeling that hits me when I open my eyes in the morning. Almost like it has broken in during the night and set up camp in my head without me even knowing.

I have had many days when I wanted to keep the curtains shut and hide from the world, days when I desperately felt like I need to tell how I feel and days when I have put on my face and continue hoping that no one would guess that I was just playing a role and that the real me was so different.

I think for me, learning to accept that this is part of who I am and that I needed to find a way to express how I feel in order to relieve myself of the muzzy feeling in my head. It was then, I picked up a pen and began to write. It soon became my medicine, my counsellor. I could scribble for hours in peace, no one to judge or interrupt and not caring what came out as it didn't matter whether it made sense to someone else. Once finished, I could shut my notebook for another day and feel that I had a listening ear, a help to clear my head.

Sometimes at night, I would lay in bed and from nowhere, words would come together in my head and a poem would be born, almost as if I already had heard it before and was just reciting it, flowing so easily. I think these times are when my best creations came together.

I do believe everyone can find a way to deal with depression, it's just a case of finding what works for you. For me, I would have been lost without my writing.

At this present time, life for me has so many more good days than dark ones. I have a wonderful partner, and children that I love dearly who have helped me continue, without even knowing it. I like myself more than I ever have and that's a good start.

Accept who you are, believe in yourself and remember, an everyday fight becomes a war if you allow it.

A Lie to Yourself

Another lie told so honestly
So much so he believes its true
You think you can smell the truth
But then wonder if it's just you.

He swears that he has been so good
And not touched a single drop
But that glaze taking over his eyes
Let's you know that he hasn't stopped.

Confrontation, followed by a barrage
Many reasons why he has slipped back
Another promise, he will try again
To get himself back on track.

This; a pattern that always repeats
As the trust disappears day by day
You find yourself always looking for signs
As the relationship is beginning to fray.

The sad thing of it all, is in all other ways
He's so loyal and loving and kind
Just such a shame at the end of each day
Only alcohol is on his mind.

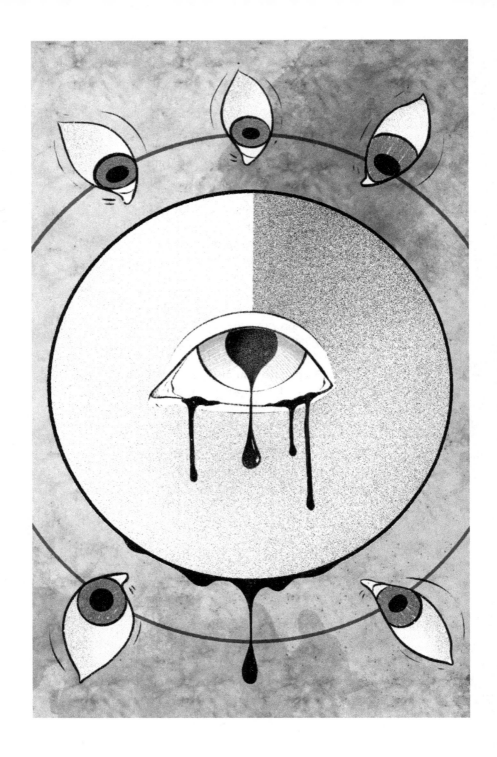

I'm Really Not

'Are you okay?' they ask me
'Of course,' I smile and say
Just don't peek through my window
Once I'm home at the end of the day.

'Are you okay? they ask me
'I'm fine,' and nod my head
Just don't feel the tears on my pillow
As I lay awake in my bed.

'Are you okay?' they ask me
'Why wouldn't I be?' I reply
Just don't study my face for too long
As I fear you will know it's a lie.

Maybe next time when they ask me
'Are you really feeling okay?'
I will open my mouth and be truthful
'No, I'm really not,' I will say.

Despair

He sat upon the soddened sand
And watched the tide withdraw
And reflected on his life's turmoil
A man who's soul was raw.

Each ripple that became a wave
Was just like his worrying mind
Crashing against the jagged rocks
Leaving such damage behind.

He looked above up at the sky
Like him, so troubled and black
A clap of lighting signalled a storm
Still he sat, no wish to head back.

And as the rain burst from its cloud
To invade his coat and find his skin
He found his whole being slowly relax
And release all the tension within.

And he howled almost as loud as the wind
As his tears danced with the rain
So many thoughts he could not talk of
For fear he was labelled insane.

The cold robbed him of his gasping breath
Waves welcomed him with evil intent
And soon he was still, at one with the sea
His time struggling with life was spent.

If only he had spoken and shared some of his pain
But mental illness is regarded as weak
Reality is your so much more of a man
If you accept your feelings and speak.

Control

How can someone steal your mind?
When its deep within your head
No longer do you have control
As it feeds on his poison instead.

He betters your brain like a strong wind
And to you, proudly exhibits his prize
Meanwhile, you slowly wither and fall
Before his cold, emotionless eyes.

The woman you once knew is left in the past
An armour of just skin and bone
The monster is laughing, picks up his crown
And takes his place high on his throne.

Like a robot you respond to every command
The praise you long for never said
Only words that cut you as sharp as knife
They degrade you and insult you instead.

Fortune

Tell me if there's a gypsy in town
Who can call me in and sit me down
She'll take my hand to read my palm
Reassure the future brings no harm.

To work her magic on my heart
Are we destined to always be apart?
To be alone for all of time
But life will go on, and I will be fine.

Maybe she will smile, look up and say
You'll find your path in your own way
Go home, be happy and be sure
You'll love again one day once more.

Money

If you had a million pounds
Would you share it all around?
Or would you hide it all away?
And save it for a rainy day.

Would you buy that new fur coat?
Maybe a castle with a moat?
A hundred or more new sports cars
Take a lifetime trip up to Mars.

If a million pounds was to be mine
Would it make my sun begin to shine?
Or stop the tears I need to cry
That's something money just can't buy.

Four Walls

This house is just four walls
But knows my secrets well
No friend of mine, no promise made
Still of them, it will not tell.

This house is just four walls
But knows the real me well
To laugh, to cry, to go insane
Still of that it will not tell.

Time

If time to think was given to you
To sort out problems and make things new
Then believe in me when I say
You'll need at least one more day!
A week, a month, maybe a year
And then who's to say it will all be clear.

Puddles

If worries were like puddles left after the rain
I would sweep them away right down the drain
Then just like the puddles, would my worries be gone?
If that's true, then I'm sure the rain won't be long.

Insecurity

Insecurity pulls you away
From you and from others
Eats away your brain
A disease out of control.

Knocks you down
All you hear is poison
Ties knots in your stomach
Plants pain in your heart.

Confidence long shattered
Love for yourself now dislike
Nothing else consumes you
And all because of something he said.

If a Book

If my life was as a book
Please turn the page and let me look
To sit and read my life away
And learn what becomes of me one day.

Of the ending will I be glad
Or maybe feel a little sad
Or shut the book for all of time
And never read the ending line.

But life's not in black and white
So, I'll carry on with this fight
And hope that things will come my way
But for now, I'll live from day by day.

If Only

If only thoughts in the brain
Would from on lips and seem the same
If only my life could be rearranged
There seems so much I need to change.

If only minds did not have circles
That spin around and play games
If only people would step forward
And take away some of this pain.

If only you could just be me
And sort this mess so I could see
And all would soon become so right
A big black hole would shed some light.

But if there is one thing, I need to learn
It's that the 'if only's', I seem to yearn
Just don't exist and that I fear
The answer lays with me right here.

Me

What would you do if I was to say?
You could be someone else for a day
Would you carry on being you?

Or maybe choose somebody new
I think I would much rather be
Anybody else but me.

Do You

When awake from a sleep
Are you glad of another day?
That brings happiness and love your way
Or do you wake to dread the start
Of another longing in your heart?

Just the Same

The wind still blows
The trees still sway
Another cold, winters day
The earth's still damp.

The sky's still grey
Another cold, winters day
The mind still spins
The worries still stay
Another cold winters day.

Another Day

One day I may smile again
Right from the heart and maybe then
I'll turn to you and say
I'm ready for another day.

One day this desk may be clear
I'm no longer sitting here
Pen and papers gone, long away
I'm ready for another day.

One day these worries are no more
I'm feeling good and secure
I can stand up with pride and say
I'm now ready for another day.

A Monster Behind
Closed Doors

I spend most days in pyjamas and a tea stained dressing gown
My hair piled up upon my head, blond but with roots of grey and brown
My acrylic nails have disappeared and what's left is flaky and thin
The waist band has expanded, so big knickers hold it all in.

The mornings where I applied my face are a distant memory
A former shadow of myself and how I used to be
The eyebrows have now mingled and have joined in matrimony
So much so, my visions blurred and I can hardly see.

The highlight of each day maybe that I have some washing to do
And for the hundredth time of the hour it seems, I make myself a brew
The hours seem to go so fast, maybe because I don't rise till late
My brain remains in lockdown mode, no need to activate.

There is no longer any reason to eagerly await the weekend
As every day is the same as they all begin to blend
So once this lockdown is over, appointments I need to make
To tame my hair, and fix those nails and stop eating cake.

There is no quick fix, but without a doubt a matter of urgency
As I fear, this lockdown monster won't be welcome back in society.

I Hand You the Crown

She controls you more than I ever could
With just a touch of your lips, no words
And that is all it seems to take
For your sense to become blurred.

To you, she offers so much support in life
Who calms you and helps with your stress
But her influence in only damaging you
And for that, she couldn't care less.

Now I can no longer compete with this love
For she has won this, hands down
So, to the best life destroyer I've ever known
Mrs Bottle, I hand you the crown.

Life

Sometimes your head don't feel right
A bit blurry, almost a haze
You know from the minute you open your eyes
It's gonna be one of those days.

So, you just want to hide away from the world
To find the time to reset your mind
But the time pounds, the nausea stays
The strength you just cannot find.

You continue your day with a smile on your face
Whilst the tears prick the black of your eyes
It's not till you're home that you allow them to flow
Where no one can hear your cries.

You know that tomorrow may bring much the same
Just hope your makeup hides what's inside
An ongoing battle within yourself
May your smile not tell them you've lied.

Hope

There's a light at the end of this tunnel
If I squint my eyes, I can see
It's far off in the distance
But it's shining just for me.

There's a light at the end of this tunnel
And although it's not very bright
I can feel its warmth and encouragement
I think I'm going to be alright.

There's a light at the end of this tunnel
I finally see which route to take
I will get to the light in this tunnel
Even if its small steps I make.

Maybe It's Over

I think I'm finally winning this fight
Or maybe we've called it a draw
Depression has downed its boxing gloves
And making its way to the door.

Slight power is starting to flood my veins
And the heaviness is leaving my mind
Self-loathing insults are breaking free
Making way for thoughts that are kind.

Oh, how I hope these feelings are true to me?
Is this battle about to end?
Finally, will I be able to feel?
That happiness could be my friend.

2020 – An Invasion

Outside it's so quiet, just the birds singing I can hear
Of this monster roaming our street, they have no idea
His armour is made of steel, and his fists are ready to fight
He is hungry to win this battle and has you in his sight.

Although you cannot see him, he's as transparent as the air
He will invade your inner organs and destroy you without a care
Oxygen and your soul to him is a banqueting feast
Not an ounce of compassion inside this mighty beast

For now, this world's in hiding, to try to save who we can
As no-one is safe from this, no woman, no child, no man
So, we stay locked in our houses, and days turn into weeks
And hope we can force this beast away from our streets

We pray the day will arrive, we can open wide our door
And walk our streets and greet our friends like we did before
To try and build our lives again, as if he had never been
This ugly, headless monster we call COVID 19.

Lose

I have so many fond memories of you
They go back so many years
To lose you was the hardest thing
I drowned in an ocean of tears.

There's so much I must thank you for
You were there along the way
And although you've gone, I feel you near
When I'm going about my day.

So grateful for the time I spent with you
While you laid so very still
I talked for a while, you breathed once more
Your passing just didn't seem real.

Now time has passed, life goes on
And I am doing the best I can
Keeping the promise, I made to you
My dearest, darling Nan.

A COVID Goodbye

She lay in her hospital bed so weak and battling for breath
Her chest rising so rapidly, she knew she was nearing her death
Her eyes shut, hand searching the blanket, hoping that someone was near
For the thought of dying alone, filled her with sadness and fear.

This virus had conquered her so quickly, determined to end her life
No concern was had for her status, as a mother, grandmother, wife
For her loved ones could not sit beside her for the virus so easily spread
So, they sat in their homes; stared at the phone, waiting, hearts full of dread.

A nurse came to sit beside her, whispered messages she was asked to pass on
Taking her hand, offering some comfort, she knew it would not be long
There she stayed till the breathing subsided and therefore free from pain
Knowing tomorrow, she'd return back to the ward and do the same over again.

CPSIA information can be obtained
at www.ICGtesting.com
Printed in the USA
LVHW080104120221
679071LV00004B/153